Trying to Catch
the Horses

Trying to Catch

the Horses

poems by Dan Gerber

Michigan State University Press
East Lansing

∞ The paper used in this publication meets the minimum require-
ments of ANSI/NISO Z39.48–1992 (R 1997) (Permanence of
Paper).

Michigan State University Press
East Lansing, Michigan 48823-5202

04 03 02 01 00 99 1 2 3 4 5 6

Library of Congress Cataloging-in-Publication Data

Gerber, Dan, 1940-
    Trying to catch the horses : poems / by Dan Gerber.
        p.   cm.
    ISBN 0-87013-534-1 (alk. paper)
    I. Title.
PS3557.E66 T79 1999
811'.54--dc21

99-6501
CIP

Grateful acknowledgment is made to the editors of the publications
in which the following poems first appeared:

"Photo of a Park in Prague" in *The Ohio Review;* "Blizzard on Dayton
Street 2:00 A.M." and "Walking Out Alone" in *New Letters;* "The Bear
on Main Street" in *GRRRRR; A Collection of Poems About Bears*
(Artcos Press); "My Father's Fields" in *The Best American Poetry 1999*
(Scribners); "Franz Kline's Dream," "Calm Spring Hours," and
"Advice from the Burglar" in *Sky;* "For Isabel" in *Grand Valley Review;*
"Psalm," "Just Before He Died," and "The Cool Earth" in *Witness;*
"My Father's Fields," "In the Still Night," and "Tarawa" in *Poetry.*

Cover Artwork "Summer Shadows Hawkwood Hill" by Carol Peek,
courtesy of the artist
Book and cover design by Michael J. Brooks

Visit Michigan State University Press on the World Wide Web at:
www.msu.edu/unit/msupress

For Debbie

and for

Dorothy Scott Merrill
1923–1998

Contemplate seeing your bodily form present before you—
in the trees, the grass and leaves, the river.

Thich Nhat Hanh

Contents

I

II

III

IV

I

Trying to Catch the Horses

When I give up and turn my attention
to the purr of the grass, the clatter of the aspen,
the clouds lifting off Mt. Teewinot,
I become a curious god, a tar baby,
a clump of grass they must graze.

I reach up and touch the blue with my fingers,
not just the air above my head,
but the sky itself as far as it goes.

Remembering to Breathe

I am entering this forest again, down a ridge of broken rock, my calves stretching with the skid of loose gravel. I pause to glance over the tops of oak and hemlock at an old burn on the far slope before I drop through dark limbs and the tick of bare branches into a mist of ferns while a breeze stirs that layer through which I descended, as if I were gazing up from the depths at waves moving over a pond.

This isn't the past, *unsunning nature*, as Emerson warned. This is the present in which a car with a blown muffler rumbles and a neighbor's dog barks.

I am finding my way now past each muscular trunk, familiar with their scars, stirring up from the sodden leaves the fragrance of a long exile.

The Trees, the Grass, the Leaves, the River

Would these things I came to praise
be pleased if I read them my poems?
Or would I feel foolish in their presence,
reciting what I've made of their incomparable lives?

If I came to this meadow to exalt them
would I clear my throat for their attention
and then be unable to speak?

Would I be wounded by the silence of the stones,
the resolve of the river,
not even pausing to listen, the falcon
intent on a life in the air, the fox
trotting off at the sound of my voice?

Or would they be secretly pleased
and reward me with their mute applause,
simply being more what they are?

Would the prairie dog come out of her den to scold me,
the crane clack and wallop her articulate wings,
the wind pick up and roar in the willows,
to absolve me in this chorus
of their amplified song?

A Tree on the Prairie in Mid-October

Something about the single aspen
I photographed a dozen times this fall,
hidden from view in sage and grass
on the far slope of the hill
I can see from my bedroom window.

Of those who walked with me,
no one took notice. I don't know why
I am drawn to this gnome-like tree,
the way its heart-shaped leaves
enliven the sun perhaps,
a little more gold each day.

Something not only of itself
comes out of the tree when I see it,
something not me that I am.

Our lives are short in the middle
and long at both ends.

How strange to give up being alone.

The Crow

I am walking on the Earth, held down
by the specifics of everything
around me. Things circle though I don't quite
perceive them as moving, except of course
the crow making lazy swats at the moment
through which he swims like a lumbering skate.

He flaps on beyond the bend of the planet,
or beyond the canyon's pine ridge
where I can no longer see him
and assume he's a prophet now, living in Judaea,
preaching to a glade in Ninevah.

Sovereign

My pickup idles, a slow gallop,
and the dog presses against my shoulder and growls
because this wolf is not of her pack,
and because this is her road home.

He holds his ground as we approach,
then turns his head mindfully
from his vigil on the evening sun,
as if we were no more than a cloud.

His brindled coat glows,
and his shoulders rise with each breath,
as utterly mysterious as my own.

I watch his yellow eyes
till he turns and crosses the road,
dragging his right hind leg.

He looks back once more from the edge of the sage.
There's nothing I can do for him,
nothing to heal his wound,
but I wish him fat field mice
and many ripe bitches,
old dog who owns my land.

Side Effects

The moon keeps the Earth on its course.
I read that. Actually, it keeps the Earth,
unlike the other planets, from wobbling,
so that we may have
somewhat predictable seasons. Hence life,
as we've come to think of it.
Steadying moon
who pulls me out to the lawn
with her light. A kind of gravity
that keeps the mad fly imprisoned by the lamp,
in spite of every effort I make to tell him
he's free to fly away.

Walking Out Alone

Have you ever doubted that the basement stairs
go deeper than the basement,
that the desire you ignore is desiring you?

That plaintive look on the faces of dogs
we take to express so much more longing
than they probably ever intended.

Beyond the meadow is a greater meadow
and beyond the trees, more trees.

In the late winter sun, these hard little pebbles
cast hard little shadows on the road.

Grouse

Grouse moving through the field this morning.
I can't really see them, still nothing else
parts the indolent grass this way.

Often, we know the world by what it isn't.
The physician on the trail of the disease.

Still, what we don't know
is subscribed by what we do. I think
this morning I'll walk the dog through that field.

Clouds

How quickly they move in
over the mountains, like a change of mood,
as I sit reading *The Death of Merlin*
or a lyric poem, though I may have read it twice,
forgetting just where the sky was.

                              Clear though,
I remember when I woke, one plume
trailing off the peak like smoke
from a latent chimney or a feather
off a pointed cap.

Only one patch of blue now,
where the sun streams through,
darkening the prairie around it.

Elements

This isn't a Disney world, but a raven came to me this morning
as if summoned. He croaked twice in flight
before landing on a fence post
not five feet from where I was sitting,
then croaked twice more to insure I'd gotten the message
before he turned and flew back to the trees.

The cranes gabble all morning,
making plans for a journey. A nervous
breeze ruffles the wings of the aspen.

The pup didn't eat her breakfast.
She sits at my feet and looks up,
trying to tell me what she doesn't understand.

The Forest Service warned me out of Badger Creek Canyon
where I fish for tiny cutthroats and dissolve my thoughts
in dissolving light.

A grizzly sow with three cubs
has repossessed my riffles and pools,
undoubtedly lured by fat autumn sheep,
down from their high summer pasture.

A week later when I venture back,
armed with bear bells and pepper spray,
I stumble on a torn fleecy carcass,
blood spattering the bankside stones
like colorless paint,
the canyon deeper than I seem to remember.

Storm Warning

I follow the trail of the deer through late summer,
or my trail the deer have claimed.

Clouds roll over me,
dragging dark islands across the plain.
Sweeps of sun on the hills.

When someone dies you can give up
making them change their mind.

The wind makes seven different sounds in the sage,
and the tall rye whips the backs of my hands.

A fly seeks shelter in my ear,
and a marsh hawk dips low,
finding a life in the ravening grass.

The Time of the Hoppers

It was August,
time of the leaping and crackling grass,
dry end of summer, of fires
and the ripening wheat.

Along the rivers the hoppers leap out with abandon,
with joy and no thought of ever coming down.
Sweeping the bank on the ride of their life,
they soon become the life of the roseate,
speckled and ravenous trout, such transformation
they never imagined.
Or maybe they had.

Who am I to speculate about the wisdom of an arthropod
I merely mimic with feathers on a hook?
Who am I to question this glorious transformation

I hold now a moment in the current
and let go

On My Walk

I wonder
if I'm any less lonely than I ever was.

Wild flowers, in this case
the yellow arrowroot,
wait for me in the fields.

The long-needled pine has secrets it will keep
till the breeze rises. And the breeze
has stories for the pine to translate.

The roots of the sage almost trip me,
and the marsh hawk swoops low
to show me her bright wings.

  She forgets she has done this before.

The fox on the hillside,
across the slim ravine, watches
to see where I might be going
and what it is I might do.

This doesn't concern her, except
that everything concerns her,
and concerns me too. I suspect

that she is always watching
and almost never lonely.

Cornhawks

The more we understand particular things,
the more we understand God.

Spinoza

This morning three cornhawks, birds
previously unknown this far west,
or east, for that matter, Descartes
was not a bad man, only
lacking the knowledge of these
inconsolable birds.

Smoke

I must have lain here a long time, in the sun, in the dry grass. I must have fallen asleep, though I don't remember waking. My dog lies curled by my thigh, and the last yellow leaves of the cottonwood tremble. Near Victor a pillar of white smoke rises from the grass and fans out against the sky. All summer the great fires in Utah and eastern Oregon softened the mountains and zeroed the sun down to a resolute ball. Our eyes watered and our noses cracked but we saw flames only on the evening news, 200,000 acres they said, in 7,400 separate fires. Before dawn I saw lights from the football field at Driggs. The potato harvest is on and the Redskins practice early to get the crop in while the weather holds. Snow already in the timberline. A ladybug inching up a long brown stalk makes a leap of faith to my knee, and a few flies buzz in the drowsy thistle heads. A pickup sweeps by down on Hatch's road, from here about the size of the ladybug it seems. Elk season, and a shot rings down from the mountain. How old is this spidery thistle branch? How many day's walk is the sea?

Counting Treasures

My dog lies on the threshold,
and her ears are never still.
If I were deaf I could read
just watching them
flag like velvet semaphores,
saying, *breeze, rain, bees,*
laughter from next door.

Pleasures

Hours squandered in the river
taxing my skill,
and a catalogue of irreconcilable desires
to deceive a fish
I have no intention of keeping.

A whole day spent
clearing twigs from the forest
for the pleasure of enjoying
a pure carpet of pine needles.

Afternoons I named every seabird
crossing the rose of my attic window,
Albert and Raoul and oafish Esmerelda
with her ponderous beak and imponderable eye.

Years spent adoring
the woman I love
simply because I adore her.

Remembering to remember, and from time to time,
remembering to water the lilacs.

On the Broad Prairie

I find myself on the broad prairie,
caught out as the sea moves under a boat,
anchored against the tide.

I set off to cross it in my summer clothes
when the season overtook me
and the Earth began its indolent slide
down the camber of an icy road.

I try walking faster, but the heat
is dying like color in the fading light.

As if we are innocent when time
takes off her girlish clothes and smiles
like a woman who knows what she's come for.

Endless Rain

It was raining in my dream,

in the dark beyond the lamp,

steady as the rocks are round,

the pool taking it in and still not overflowing.

Being and non-being are all the same.

The sky is immense and impossible.

My life dims down to this room in November.

The world is an adjective.

The shadow can't quite live alone.

The rain keeps on falling, and the dark streets
glisten.

The Bear on Main Street

What made the man kill this bear?
His truck, across which the bear's body lies,
tells me it wasn't to feed his family
or because his children were cold.

The bear has beautiful black feet, delicate
almost, like the soles of patent leather slippers,
and the wind riffles the surface of its fur
with the sheen of water in the autumn sun.

The bear looks as if it might only be sleeping,
but its tongue lags from its mouth, and the man
has wrapped it with stout twine and bound it
to the bed of his truck,
as if he were afraid it might speak.

Three teenage boys pull their pickup to the curb.
One of the boys guesses what the bear must weigh.
Another wants to know how many shots it took,
and the third boy climbs down. He strokes its nose and forehead.
He traces the bear's no longer living skull
with the living bones of his fingers
and wonders by what impossible road
he will come to his father's country.

The River Seen from Above

It's very difficult to look at the world
and into your heart at the same time.

Jim Harrison

We see the man walking toward the edge,
the thin crust he doesn't see.
A spring day in mid-winter. He, and we, can feel
the returning heat of the sun, smell the loam
so long frozen, the fresh basil from memory,
expecting the *twer* of a blackbird with each step.

How cruel to come in
so close to the end of this beautiful movie,
how cruel to see this direction
and be unable to change it,
this abundant life so near its conclusion.

Our conclusion, though perhaps, not his.

II

Tarawa

they did not hear the singing of the reefs long enough
and perhaps never touched the islands,
those wreaths of brilliance and perfume,
except to die:

Pablo Neruda

This is a story about what happened in '43-
there are twenty thousand and twenty-seven
stories like this—about the hit I took
through the knee on the way in,
wading over the long reef,
about the color of the water
around me, how it blended
with bits of broken coral
and blood from other knees, like a great soup
stirred up from leftovers, how the frightened bonefish
trapped by the tide,
shot through our legs. We never thought
of fish in the sea and how
this was their home though not their war,
and not ours either, though
we were swimming in it.

Express

A man collapses on the seat next to mine.
He is struggling for breath.
He must have run the length of the platform
as the train was leaving the station.
He is dressed much as I am,
though his shirt is rumpled and darkened with sweat.

He turns to me with a pleading expression.
He tells me I am lucky. I wonder
at first if he's brought me some news. A little steam
drifts by the window, and we're well out,
clear of the city now. I want to ask him
what he means by "lucky,"
but I see him drifting off,
and a smile has softened his face.

We're rushing ahead into unknown country
on a well-worn track. This man,
so like me, is having a dream.

South of Marrakech

He remembers the car on its smashed roof,
wheels up, like a sleeping dog,
the dark, almost colorless rocks,
before the heat of the morning,
the men in their musty djellabahs
around the small fire, cooking coffee
by the road to Ait Benhaddou,
the bodies half covered, the surprisingly delicate
foot of the woman and the blue-stained arm of the man,
blood sticky in the cupped palm of his hand,
coffee coming to a boil in the tall brass pot,
the man with the milky eye gesturing
toward the cloudless sky
when we stopped because we were strangers,
to see what there was we might do.

In the Still Night

Animals walk into the open notebook before him.
A woman walks in.
Night casts its mothy light
on the pages. His words
shine like black pebbles
through a still, almost imperceptible stream,
and a tree rises up
out of pressed fiber, its roots
enclosing his chest.

The tree darkens in the coming storm
as if the earth welled up in its leaves
like blood in a face dark with longing.

He sketches a savannah with lions
asleep in the shade of this anvil-shaped tree,
and appearing just now as a whirl in the long grass,
his imagination moves toward them
like the name of rain in a dry season.

One Day Near Marilal

for Lambat

We needed meat for the camp, and
never having killed anything big, I wanted
to know what it meant to skin and clean a life,
and to eat it to stay alive.

But this death would have been too easy,
this beautiful impala, this *dúme*,
who presented himself in the first half hour
as though it had all been arranged.

I eased the rifle down.

This wasn't what I thought it would be,
I told Bill. I would only do this once,
and there had to be more to it than this.

But in our tracker's black face, a black rage was growing.
You go back to America, he said.
You take pictures.

This *dúme* would have been dinner for us all.

He doesn't want to kill something like an impala.
Something beautiful. Bill tried to explain.
He wants to kill something ugly,
like a wart hog.

The tracker drew himself up like a cobra
and looked off toward the afternoon hills.

Beautiful, he said, as if a word to learn.
Beautiful or ugly, the heart is one.

Dúme (do-may): the Swahili word for the male of the herd

Flight

She told me no man
ever pleased her this way
and asked sweetly
if I would do it again.

Of course I was really pleasing myself,
the way raptors are pleased
by the air moving under their wings,
only more so
when the wind they create buffets back
with its own life,
and the trailing feathers thrill
to this unbidden lift.

Photo of a Park in Prague

No one is visible at the moment.
The upturned wheelbarrow rests on the walk,
and the pail is perched on the wall.

The morning mist has risen
from a scattering of brittle leaves
to those not yet brittle on the trees

and may rest, at the moment, on the sleeve
of whoever has departed
and may soon re-enter.

The pail, dwarfed by a rococo urn,
appears to enclose the roots of a willow
at the distant edge of the lawn,

an illusion that may be a flaw
a slight move to left would correct.

But no movement's allowed at the moment.

A Geography of Being

A tool I find myself at the moment
unable to locate in my toolbox.

Language is such an immanent thing.
Even poets admit

there's more than one way,
except for what can't be said.

A thousand revisions make it
just about right.

Our perceptions
alter what we think of the landscape.

One storm
can change it completely.

Being keeps us in place,
more or less. Here

is there from over there
but never from here,

as far as we know.

In the mountains I see the world
as mountains.

On the sea I notice the clouds.

Under the Great Sky

A letter in the hold of a 757
leaps over six hundred million hours
of being, a simultaneous aeon,
to say I love you, or
please sign the enclosed and return.

The postman steps out of the elevator
and through the revolving door.

The letter is read and reread,
then pressed in the leaves of a book.

Or maybe it's returned.

Franz Kline's Dream

The train is stalled on the siding.
No news about the delay.
Some say it's political, a strike or
a shipment of strategic material.

Word spreads of an earthquake in the country ahead.
Word spreads of a war. Someone says
it's a drug bust. No one would suspect
the trains.

Maybe we've simply been tabled he thinks,
life's spillover sloughed off like yeast.
He tries to recall a verse or a prayer.
A single name will do.

It's dark out there,
no lights from a town or farm,
no eternal stars, nothing
to give us a place but snow
as the ground for this one dark track.

Adrift

There was nothing he could do now, nothing
to provide for his journey. And so
doing nothing was easy.

The boat without power would go
where the current took it, the falling tide
drawing him out to where
the horizon would be.

                    But the light from the clouds
hammered it smooth like fine metal
hammered into leaf on an anvil
between ocean and what the sky might bring.

The woman he would never see again,
a creature as the sharks are
creatures, and the tern alone so high,
a spirit alone for all he could see.

And he noticed a large green turtle
lolling in the swells,

how he would tell
of its large dispassionate eye,

how it calmed him to someone
he had the chance to be someday.

One Drop of Crocodile

What could the lizard on the path be thinking
as he strips off and eats his own skin,
the way I sometimes nibble at my sunburned lips?

He wolfs down a gossamer sheet from his back
like sugared phyllo dough,
then bends his neck back to devour a knee cap,
unless an ant or a moth or his newly hatched nephew
comes along.

It's all the same to this teardrop tyrannosaurus,
who swallows and blinks and flexes his throat.

He is the life of the life we've been promised.

And what more could I ask, here in my garden,
now that it's almost June?

Spring Song in Key West

This place where bird songs are rare in spring.
Only the catbird in her glorious, confused aria,
blossoms from the sapodilla now and then,
and the osprey whistling far above from the sea,
and the wild parrots assaulting our trees
again each year without warning
of some end they say is
coming,   coming.

Calm Spring Hours

after Juan Ramón Jiménez

These calm spring hours make us homesick
for what we haven't lost.
Or is this what love is?
The drone of an airplane hidden by clouds?

III

The Cool Earth

It's noontime on a summer day sometime around 1948. Boxcars are standing on the tracks, doors open, waiting for the rest of their loads. But it's noontime now and the lift truck drivers are resting. Hay bales stretch out over half the field. The farm hands are resting under the large maple along the fence line, their shirts wet from the morning's hauling, and with the light breeze there in the shade, the rough cotton feels cold against their backs and ribs. I come home, hot from play. My mother has made me an egg salad sandwich, and the screen door whaps on its spring. Our dog is resting on the cool earth of the foxhole he's scooped out against the foundation of the house. My father stops to speak to him before he comes in. My father groans as he imagines he would groan if he were the dog, stretching there to his greeting, stiff legged on the cool black earth in the shadow of the kitchen roof. He carries the jacket of his seersucker suit on his arm, and the morning's mail in his hand. There is a knowing, beyond but not apart from this. I hear the *braang* of the spring as it stretches, though there is no slap, as my father eases the door shut behind him. He kisses my mother and drops the mail on the counter. "It's hot," he says, but he clearly enjoys it. He's as happy as I am that it's a hot summer day in our little town and that it's noontime sometime around 1948.

Blackbirds

For almost a month it's forgotten to be spring,
as if rehearsing in a hall next door,
a concert that could open any day now.

Spirit Harness

It is a long black bridge,
So long that to cross it is unthinkable.
Shinkichi Takahashi

But before I set foot on it, I realize
I am already on the other side.

Though I can never cross it, the bridge
is there like a finger pointing at the moon,

though the finger itself gives off no light.

The March of Time

I never draw nearer the Future.
The Future draws nearer to me, as if,
cold in eternal abstraction,
it longs for some animal to devour,
some human warmth to save it
from never coming to be.

The Past comes to me, and I
meet it halfway. More than that,
it begs me to spend the night,
take a month's lease. A year.
Don't ever leave me my darling,
it cries.
I made you all you are today.
Don't ever think you can leave me behind.
Please,
don't ever think that.

Trust Account

What we are trusts us to trust it.
The window, an eye
through which we may see
the door, a portal to leave the past,
the hinge, a bend upon which
so much hinges.

If this sounds redundant then
life is redundant,
on scant evidence, something
that never should have been. But here

we are talking about trust,
giving up the need to be one thing only,
the cloud, its fear of being rain,
the leaf of being compost and the compost
of becoming a leaf. We are
the life of a great machine, the magician
transmuting the lady into a leopard.
Only how much more amazing,
the magician transmuting himself
into us.

Just Before He Died

My father told me all he would miss
was that Hungarian stew my mother was cooking
the evening I took him to the hospital.
Years have passed now. My mother
dead for a decade. I wonder
if he really did miss that pungent stew?
I wonder if he still does?
I wonder if she brought it in a golden bowl?
Or if he turned, as a child
turns to other things,
like the first glimpse of mountains,
driving west?

Psalm

All my dead are with me.
All my dead are at ease,
free of time and what never may be.
All my dead are at peace with each other.
They will never change their minds.
They forgive me whatever I feel
needs forgiveness, and blame
what I think needs blame.
They are sunlight come to comfort me.
They lead me on the trail of my life's work.
In my hand I see my father's hand,
holding this pen.
My mother's eyes, finally free of longing,
gaze at me from the mirror.
When I stand they look up
to see where I'm going.
They can't see far through the tall grass,
but they see the tall grass,
and they smile to see it moving behind me.

For Isabel

Genocide in Rwanda, and we are in love.
Our love, your's and mine, can't stop it,

can't bring peace to Palestine or justice
to the Muslims and Serbs, can't even

balance the budget or cure any one
of the four thousand twenty-seven diseases.

Yet we go on loving each other, the garden,
and, by extension, the gardener, the house

and the woman who cleans it. Like a blotter
absorbing spilled ink, the borders blur,
like old maps before there were countries.

Like old lives from the viewpoint of atoms.

Dust

This crumbling brick has no fear of death,
doesn't know if it's coming or going.

Particles compressed make a brick,
make the brick, like me,
an assemblage.

Speck of dust, who are you?
Never again will I shake out the rag,
determined to be rid of you once and for all.

Where have you been my love?
And where will I meet you tomorrow?

Sometimes

Somewhere in a desert the one we hoped to be
is rescued by the one we hoped to leave behind.

It takes a life to prepare us for living,
the same mistakes in new garb.

We lift the sword to fend off a blow
and clip the one we love on the chin.

Our eyes are the treasure for which we are looking,
and that bad smell, the shit that sticks to our nose.

IV

A Sport Almost

> . . . *the fate of poetry is to fall in love with the world,*
> *in spite of history.*
>
> Derek Walcott

The Lakota made war, or skirmish,
a way of proving valor,
free of scorched earth and pestilence,
a land belonged to with their lives.

Labels and broken glass, last traces
of snow in the sun and new grass
along the highway south of Chadron.

When we stop to pee in the roadside wild hemp,
I see the bright, faint silver of cranes overhead,
carrying the latest news of Matamoros
to the still rising fields of Wyoming.

Miles into western South Dakota,
we talk about emptiness and causes,
what we have given for what we have.
How loneliness is the stepchild of
loneliness, you said.

On the fence line, above a ravine,
I notice two horses
leave their grazing and pick up their heads.
Mute companions in their freedom,
aching like swans,
awaiting our arrival it seems.

Blizzard on Dayton Street 2:00 A.M.

The power is out, and this storm
wipes out all the givens,
debts, fears, taxes, and jealousies
that make our lives so intriguing.

Snow plumes off the dark roofs
like the South Col of K2,
houses edging over their lot lines
majestic and implacable
on the night harbor,
maneuvering for position, the first salvos
about to rip through the attic gables.

Sexual

The word attacks the page again and again.
Looks for a hold to absorb it.
Ink fills up the porous wells, pools
up inside like the sea.

A pale birdcry where
no bird should be.

If you tell me the river is here
I will ask you which river.
Not its name; I ask you
which river?

Advice from the Burglar

Sometimes the most audacious attempt
is the only way in,
when all the other windows are shuttered
and only that one on the street,
so naked in the light,
no one would think to defend it.

Go about this as if you belong here.
Bring your ladder.
Bring music and all your tools.
And make a neat job of it.
Talk with anyone who stops.
Speak of the weather and how you'd rather be sailing.

The tricky part comes once you're inside.
Others may have tried this before you.
The house seems familiar, and the owner
may have left something for you.

It may, in fact, be what you're seeking.

The Favorite Child

*My mother cries because I am old in my time
and because I will never be old enough to be old in hers.*
                                        Céasar Vallejo

When your mother, in the pale moonlight,
bent down to your cradle and whispered
This child is my favorite,
you might have heard another voice
singing like a kettle of steam,

*And I'll caress him when he pleases me
and teach him everything I know, almost,
and make him love the things I love.*

*And he will be my longing
for a place I'll never be,
and I will be the smile
of a woman he'll never know.*

*And I will eat this child, and he will satisfy
the hunger in me. Maybe.
And I will eat him slowly, a little
at a time and make him last
my whole long life, and even a little longer
so that I can go on eating
even when I have no stomach.*

The Tongue in Praise of Itself

The tongue is an articulate companion,
good for conversation and dining in,
a shrewd help in the kitchen
for advice about oregano and advice
not even desired. It will speak,
its anger unbidden. Sometimes
it gets acid and can't even be held.
Difficult to comfort but often
a comfort to others, it brings
pleasure through deception
though deception we hear
is a relative thing. The tongue
gives in and gives out, the sole
receptor that works it both ways,
though merely hinged at one end.

If you're hearing this now
you are hearing in English;
if French, I am
speaking in tongues.

Lost on the Mountain Above Snake Creek

The only way I know being down
through lodgepole and Douglas fir, eventually
a few aspen where the scree gives way,
close enough now
to hear the rushing water,
no more concerned
with continuing than the river.

A night bird I never thought to name,
privileged to her hunger,
as she pulled me to the mattress
with her hands and gaze.

I didn't ask whether
it was worth the effort, knowing

if you don't leave now,
you can't come back.

Quite by Chance

I find myself by a lake
where I discover my divorced wife,
long dead now,
spent her summers as a child,
long before I knew her name.

I loved that little girl
I never knew. I must have
because I later loved the woman
those summers became.

I must still love her in some way or why
does this knowing become such sweet pain—
something I think I want to tell the little girl
who of course has been well warned
not to speak to strangers.

A Face at the Window

Old sorrows that lurk around the house,
feeling for a crack in the siding,
are like a fire we think has gone cold,
the embers ground into ashes
but the ashes still glow.

They wait in the dark till we're distracted,
then slip in around a casement
where we've let the caulking go.

We sit them down at our table
without thinking. We warm them
with our desires; we tell them our favorite stories
and urge them to drink our best wine.

We embrace them and they
whisper the names that have wronged us.
We feel them breathe in our ear
and grow dizzy with their love of injustice.

They form to our bodies like worn leather
till we hardly sense them at all,
only that the night has grown thicker
and the lamplight strains at the bulb.

I think of Orpheus coming out of that darkness
with nothing but tears to show for his travail,
that what we still long for
longs to be let go,
like that fleeting but unmistakable flavor in the air
just before it starts to rain.

Plum Rain

The final plum in the kitchen bowl,
overripe, its skin even a little withered,
but sweet, so sweet it breaks in two
as I bite into it. The pit, like the soul
that isn't inside the body
but still is the body,
pops out into my fingers,
and the short stem
I fish from between my teeth
points back to the tree,
the sun and the rain
where the plum and I
began this fatal longing.

My Father's Fields

September 1918

They looked like blackbirds, my father said,
that first burst of shrapnel,
spiraling up in autumn flight,
and at first that's what he thought they were,
their glossy wings catching the sun
as they wheeled in the morning sky.

There was that moment of beauty,
the glint of it,
in that first day on the Meuse-Argonne
before the Earth came off its perch,
as if they had offended it somehow,
or that's the thought he had, he said,
the Earth rising up over every stored transgression,
and what had they done to bring this on?

Later it was all the dead horses,
the field before the river strewn with horses,
and his friend, Carl Johnson,
sleeping off the numbness of battle,
at peace almost,
but for the way his leg wrapped up behind him,
and the too-wide smile
of the bloody mouth across his neck,
Carl playing dead among the horses; he thought
of Carl with his Belgians at the county fair.

90,000 horses moving up the roads at night.
He'd never imagined so many horses
in the history of the world,
or so many men in their silent march,
imagining no longer, the September morning
as they looked out on the manicured stubble
of the burnt-gold fields
and the still green trees in the haze
along the river.

These few things he noted in his journal,
though he spoke to me only of the horses,
the things people said, and the newly shorn fields.

The trees along the river are what I see
when I think my father's thoughts,
not the fiery sky, the tangled wire,
the splintered forest or all the dead horses,
but those fields shorn of wheat,
as his father's fields would be in September.

Wild Horses

Out my window, wild horses. Or they aren't really wild; they are my neighbor's horses wandering over the unfenced fields. They are wild to me. They touch something long before monoxodil and the World Wide Web. *To see you naked is to see the Earth swept clean of horses.* But not really; swept clean *for* horses maybe. My neighbor's daughter rolls down the car window to ask if I've seen her horses. One of them is black and white. Something in me wants her to ask me to saddle up and help her corral them. To ride down the scree slopes of canyons, to come into a wild country where the centaur still lives, to ride together till *the hills run away.* I tell her I saw them move off over Teton Ridge, southeast. Good luck I tell her. She backs on the shoulder and waves as she turns toward home. Wild horses. One of them a paint with a black fiddle head. I look back over my shoulder. I can smell the riders coming. I wait for them on the ridge above the coulee. I will let them come closer, to almost believe they can catch me.

Books by Dan Gerber

Poetry

The Revenant
Departure
The Chinese Poems
Snow on the Backs of Animals
A Last Bridge Home: New and Selected Poems

Novels

American Atlas
Out of Control
A Voice from the River

Short Stories

Grass Fires

Nonfiction

Indy: The World's Fastest Carnival Ride

Dan Gerber was born and grew up in western Michigan and earned his B.A. from Michigan State University in 1962. He has worked as a corporate executive, an automobile dealer, a professional racing driver, and a high school teacher. From 1968 through 1972, with Jim Harrison, he co-edited the literary magazine *Sumac*. He has traveled extensively as a journalist, particularly in Africa. He has been writer-in-residence at Michigan State University and Grand Valley State College and has lectured, read, and taught at numerous colleges, universities, libraries, schools, and museums throughout the United States and England. He has been nominated for a Pushcart Prize, won the 1992 Michigan Author Award, and has had work selected for *The Best American Poetry 1999*. He and his wife Debbie divide their year between central California and southeastern Idaho.